Charities

Teaching Tips

Gold Level 9
This book focuses on developing reading independence, fluency, and comprehension.

Before Reading
- Ask readers what they think the book will be about based on the title. Have them support their answer.

Read the Book
- Encourage readers to read silently on their own.
- As readers encounter unfamiliar words, ask them to look for context clues to see if they can figure out what the words mean. Encourage them to locate boldfaced words in the glossary and ask questions to clarify the meaning of new vocabulary.
- Allow readers time to absorb the text and think about each chapter.
- Ask readers to write down any questions they have about the book's content.

After Reading
- Ask readers to summarize the book.
- Encourage them to point out anything they did not understand and ask questions.
- Ask readers to review the questions on page 23. Have them go back through the book to find answers. Have them write their answers on a separate sheet of paper.

© 2024 Booklife Publishing
This edition is published by arrangement with Booklife Publishing.

North American adaptations © 2024 Jump!
5357 Penn Avenue South
Minneapolis, MN 55419
www.jumplibrary.com

Library of Congress Cataloging-in-Publication Data is available at www.loc.gov or upon request from the publisher.

ISBN: 979-8-88996-915-0 (hardcover)
ISBN: 979-8-88996-916-7 (paperback)
ISBN: 979-8-88996-917-4 (ebook)

Decodables by Jump! are published by Jump! Library.
All rights reserved. No part of this book may be reproduced in any form without written permission from the publisher.

Photo Credits
Images are courtesy of Shutterstock.com. With thanks to Getty Images, Thinkstock Photo and iStockphoto. Cover – deryabinka. p4–5 – Hurst Photo, Monkey Business Images. p6–7 – Mila Supinskaya Glashchenko, Roger de la Harpe. p8–9 – Leonid Sorokin, Pornpimon Ainkaew. p10–11 – Dennis Diatel, Dmytro Zinkevych. p12–13 – Matej Kastelic, tilialucida. p14–15 – Blue Planet Studio, Veja_shutterstock. p16–17 – Gail Johnson, sJH Bispo. p18–19 – Don Mammoser, XiXinXing. p20–21 – Monkey Business Images, Anita van den Broe.

Table of Contents

Page 4   What Is a Charity?

Page 6   Animal Charities

Page 8   Environmental Charities

Page 10   Human Charities

Page 12   Medical Charities

Page 14   How Do Charities Raise Money?

Page 16   How Animal and Environmental Charities Spend Money

Page 18   How Human and Medical Charities Spend Money

Page 20   How You Can Help

Page 22   Index

Page 23   Questions

Page 24   Glossary

What Is a Charity?

A charity is an organization that supports animals, people, or causes that need help. Within a charity, people work hard to help make something in the world better.

People who work for a charity without being paid are called volunteers.

There are thousands of charities around the world. Each charity helps a different group in need. Charities do not make a profit. This means the charity does not keep any of the money it makes.

Animal Charities

Animals need food, water, and **shelter** to stay alive and healthy. Many animals do not have these things. Some animals need protection from dangers caused by humans, such as hunting.

Some humans hunt black rhinos for their horns.

Some animal charities look after animals that have not been cared for properly, such as unwanted pets. An animal's natural home is called its habitat. Some charities work to protect habitats so that animals can continue to live in them.

Environmental Charities

The environment is made up of all natural things. **Pollution** and **climate change** are damaging it. If the environment is not protected, plant, animal, and human life may suffer.

This factory is creating pollution.

Environmental charities teach people how to protect our planet and look after natural places. Some charities carry out **research** to help us understand the natural world. Some groups organize **protests** to try and stop things that damage the environment.

Human Charities

People need food, clean water, clothing, and shelter. Everyone needs **health care** and safety from danger. Some people do not have these things.

Many people have to travel a long way to get clean water to drink.

Human charities work to make sure everyone has the things they need. Some charities give people food and clean water. Other charities help people who are not safe in their homes. Some even build schools for children.

Medical Charities

Medical charities carry out important research. This research helps scientists learn about **diseases**. It helps them find cures and treatments. Lots of equipment is needed to do medical research, so it can cost a lot of money.

Many medical charities work with scientists to make medicines. Other charities give money to people who are affected by a disease. Some medical charities teach people about diseases, such as what causes them, and what to do in an emergency.

How Do Charities Raise Money?

Charities raise money by asking for **donations**. They often use **advertisements** on television, online, or on the radio to ask for help. Some people donate a certain amount of money to a charity each month.

Some people take part in fundraising events, such as **marathons**, to raise money for charity. People can also donate things they no longer want to charity stores. The stores raise money by selling these things to other people.

How Animal and Environmental Charities Spend Money

Animal charities may use their money to give animals food, shelter, and medicine. Some charities organize workshops that teach people about animals and how to protect them.

This donkey lives in a safe place called a sanctuary.

Some environmental charities work to protect natural spaces. Other charities pay for projects that help people live in environmentally friendly ways. For example, they help people grow crops in ways that do not harm rain forests.

How Human and Medical Charities Spend Money

Human charities use their money to buy things that the people they are helping need, such as food and clothing. Some charities buy special equipment, such as mosquito nets or water pumps, for people to use.

Mosquito nets protect people from dangerous insect bites.

Medical charities use money to pay for important research and equipment. Some charities set up programs that care for people near the end of their lives. Other charities pay nurses to look after people who are sick.

How You Can Help

There are lots of ways you can help charities. First, try and find out as much as you can about what different charities do and why their work is important. Which charity would you like to support?

You could help charities with donations. You could donate money, clothes, food, or toys that you do not need or want. Are there any charity fundraising events near you? If not, you could organize your own fundraising event!

Index

habitats 7
money 5, 12–16, 18–19, 21
mosquito nets 18
protests 9
water 6, 10–11, 18

How to Use an Index

An index helps us find information in a book. Each word has a set of page numbers. These page numbers are where you can find information about that word.

Page numbers

Example: balloons 5, 8–10, 19

Important word

This means page 8, page 10, and all the pages in between. Here, it means pages 8, 9, and 10.

Questions

1. What is the name for a person who works for a charity without getting paid?

2. Why does medical research cost a lot of money?

3. What is one way you could help charities?

4. Using the Table of Contents, can you find which pages have information about how charities raise money?

5. Using the Index, can you find a page in the book about mosquito nets?

6. Using the Glossary, can you define what climate change is?

Glossary

advertisements:
Notices to the public that bring attention to a cause or event.

climate change:
Changes in Earth's weather and climate over time.

diseases:
Illnesses.

donations:
Gifts, such as money, given to charities.

health care:
Medical services.

marathons:
Races during which people run for long stretches of time.

pollution:
Harmful substances, such as chemicals, that hurt the water, air, and soil.

protests:
Public demonstrations that oppose something.

research:
A study or investigation in a particular field to learn new facts or solve a problem.

shelter:
A place that provides safety and protection.